THE NOVELIZATION

Published in 1994 by Grosset & Dunlap, Inc., a member of The Putnam & Grosset Group, New York. GROSSET & DUNLAP is a trademark of Grosset & Dunlap, Inc. Published simultaneously in Canada. Printed in the U.S.A.
Library of Congress Catalog Card Number: 93-80897   ISBN 0-448-40726-4
A B C D E F G H I J

THE NOVELIZATION

ADAPTED BY FRANCINE HUGHES
BASED ON A SCREENPLAY WRITTEN BY
TOM S. PARKER & JIM JENNEWEIN
AND STEVEN E. DE SOUZA

GROSSET & DUNLAP ◆ NEW YORK

CHAPTER 1

A long time ago...in the prehistoric Stone Age...in a prehistoric valley...by a prehistoric mountain...was a prehistoric town. Bedrock.

Bedrock had an airport. Pterodactyl planes took off every hour on the hour. It had a drive-in movie theater. *Tar Wars* was playing. Bedrock had a RocDonald's fast-food restaurant, stores, and offices. It even had a rock quarry, Slate and Co., where workers made houses from stone.

At the rock quarry, Cliff Vandercave was looking down at the workers from his high-rise office. As he watched, the workers used axes and hammers to hollow out a giant boulder. Then they cut out windows and a door. Finally, they heaved a heavy roof into place. The workers sweated and strained ...and at last! A complete stone-age home was finished. But Cliff was not impressed. He was laughing at all their hard work.

"Look at those stupid worms, working their lives away," he said to his secretary. Cliff was a vice president at Slate and Co. Construction. He had a tan, an expensive suit, and a smile that was 100 percent phony. And he never worked hard.

"Do you know why I'm up here and they're down there, Miss Stone?"

Miss Stone, his secretary, was pretty and smart. She smiled at Cliff. "Because you lied on your job application?" she said.

"No . . . because I have a vision. I see things. Right now I see you and me skipping town with Mr. Slate's money. And somewhere down there"— Cliff pointed to the quarry workers—"is the stupid slob who will make it all come true."

Down in the quarry, Fred Flintstone was working his bronto-crane. He pulled one lever. The brontosaurus bit into a heavy boulder and lifted it off the ground. Fred pulled another lever. Boom! The brontosaurus dropped the boulder in a different spot.

Fred sighed. He tugged at his turtle-shell hardhat. He was tired of working. Would this day ever end?

Just then, the construction foreman pulled the Whistlebird's tail. "WOOOHHH!" the bird cried out. Fred was finished for the day.

"Yabba-dabba-dooooooo!" he shouted, jumping off the bronto's back, and sliding down its long tail.

Fred flew off the brontosaurus—right into his stone-age car. He put his two feet on the ground and began to walk. Left foot, right foot. Left foot, right foot. Quicker and quicker. The car was picking up speed. Fred couldn't wait to get home!

Fred drove to the quarry gate. Then he put his stone time card up to the stegosaurus time clock. The stegosaurus opened its mouth wide. Crunch! Fred was punched out. And just in time to pick up Barney Rubble, his best friend and next-door neighbor.

"Hey, Fred," Barney said on their way home. "I have to tell you. I'm so excited! I'm going to be a father. I still can't believe it. Imagine! Betty and me adopting a son. A son named Bamm-Bamm! We owe it all to you, Fred. You gave us the money to make it possible. And I want the world to know it!"

Fred frowned. "Now, Barney. Remember. Me giving you that money? That's just between us. Seeing your happiness is enough for me!"

Barney nodded. He understood. Fred was afraid to tell his wife.

CHAPTER 2

A few minutes later, Fred and Barney were driving down their street. It was a quiet, tree-lined block. Fred waved at the kids playing basketrock. He said hello to a neighbor mowing his lawn with a lobster. It was good to be home.

After saying good-bye to Barney, Fred opened the door to his stone-age house.

"Wilma!" he called to his wife. "I'm home!"

Dino, the pet dinosaur, jumped to his feet. Fred was home! He charged straight over.

Fred saw the big dinosaur heading right for him. "No, Dino!" he cried. "Heel!" But it was too late. Thud! Fred was already flat on his back. And Dino was standing on top of him, licking his face with his giant tongue.

"Yuck!" said Fred, pushing him off.

Then, feeling a little shaky, Fred got to his feet. "Hi, Wilma," he said. "I didn't see you there, behind Dino."

Wilma was carrying their two-year-old daughter Pebbles.

"Da-da, home!" said Pebbles.

Fred smiled. He loved his family more than anything in the world. "Here comes the big daddy-saurus," he said, taking Pebbles in his arms and kissing her.

Now it was time for Fred to relax. He sat back in his Bark-o'-Lounger chair, and picked up a big stone slab. It was a copy of *The Bedrock News*. Wilma came over with his slippers and a pillow. Life is good, Fred thought, leaning back.

He was only half-listening to Wilma telling him about her day. But then, something she said made him sit up straight.

"The garbage disposal broke down," she was saying. "I needed money to buy a new one. So I went to the bank—"

The bank! Fred leaped to his feet. There wasn't any money in the bank. Fred had given it all to Barney!

"We don't need a new disposal," he said, rushing to the kitchen. "There's nothing wrong with this one." Fred looked under the sink. The Pigasaurus garbage disposal looked back. Fred shook his head. The Pigasaurus did seem kind of sick.

So Fred went to work. He reached into the Pigasaurus's mouth. There was a clog in there somewhere, and Fred had to fix it.

"Fred. About the money—" Wilma was standing over him. Fred pretended to be so busy, he didn't hear.

"Fred?" Finally, Wilma crossed her arms. "Fred, where's our money?" she said sternly. She wanted an answer. And she wanted it now.

"Now see here, Wilma." Fred pulled a fork out of the Pigasaurus's mouth, and stood up to face his wife. "In this house, I am king . . ." Fred took one look at Wilma's angry face ". . . and you have every right to know about the money, my queen. I gave it to Barney."

"What!" said Wilma. She couldn't believe it! Their life savings was gone. And Barney had it?

"Wilma, that money helped them adopt Bamm-Bamm. So go ahead. Scream. Yell. Let the fur fly."

Wilma started toward Fred. And she gave him a big hug.

The next day, the Rubbles went to the adoption agency. They were finally bringing Bamm-Bamm home.

"He's been raised by mastodons," the worker at

the adoption agency explained as she brought out Bamm-Bamm. "So he might be a little wild."

Bamm-Bamm was carrying a club. He had long, dirty hair. He looked like a ferocious little cave boy. And when he saw the strangers in the room, he gave a low growl.

"Oh, Barney. Isn't he precious?" Betty cooed.

Snip, snip. Betty cut Bamm-Bamm's hair as soon as they got home. Then she put him in the kitchen sink for his very first bath. A mastodon was waiting outside the window. Whoosh! Water poured out of the mastodon's trunk. It streamed through the open window, into the sink, and all over Bamm-Bamm.

When Bamm-Bamm was clean and dry, Barney took him into the yard. He wanted to play ball with his son. Very softly, so Bamm-Bamm wouldn't get hurt, Barney tossed him the ball.

Bamm-Bamm picked it up, and threw it back. Hard. The ball sped toward Barney. Barney caught it. But it was going so fast, it knocked him off his feet. Barney went flying across the yard.

"Bamm-bamm!" said Bamm-Bamm.

Sitting up, Barney rubbed his head happily. Bamm-Bamm's the perfect son, he thought. And he had the perfect family. Thanks to his best buddy, Fred.

CHAPTER 3

A few nights after that, Fred and Barney headed to the Bedrock Bowl-O-Rama. The two friends belonged to a lodge called The Royal Order of the Water Buffalo. Tonight was extra-special. Fred and Barney's lodge was having a bowling tournament. The Water Buffalos were playing the Missing Links for the championship.

"Okay, Brother Flintstone," Barney said, slapping Fred on the back. It was the last frame in a very close game. "We need a strike to win. Can you do it?"

"Is the earth flat?" Fred said, sounding very sure of himself.

Fred hefted the heavy stone bowling ball. He checked the alley. The ball. The wind. Finally, he was ready.

Fred stood up on his tippy-toes. He swung back the ball. Quickly, he tiptoed forward and let go. Fred grinned. His "twinkle toes" technique never failed.

Clunk, clunk, clunk. The ball bounced down the lane. It was heading straight for the left gutter. So Fred twisted his whole body to the right. The ball curved right. But now it was heading toward the right gutter. Fred groaned, and twisted his body left. The ball curved left . . . and bam . . . it hit the pins.

Strike! The Water Buffalos had won the tournament!

Barney and the lodge brothers gathered around Fred.

"I'd like to propose a toast," Barney announced. "To Fred Flintstone. He's not only a great bowler. He's a great human being, too."

Barney took a deep breath and began to recite:

"Since I was just a lad of ten,
I've had the very bestest friend.
He may be big, he may be loud.
So you'll never lose him in a crowd.
But for my friend, the special part
Is what's behind his ribs —
his heart."

Fred sniffled. He was so moved! Big elephant tears rolled down his cheeks. But Barney wasn't through yet.

> "I owe my son to him and now,
> I stand before my peers and vow
> I'll pay him back someday,
> somehow.
> The end."

By now, Fred was standing in a puddle of tears. "That was beautiful, Barney," he said, stepping out of the water to shake his friend's hand. "Just beautiful."

When the victory party was over, Fred went home and tiptoed inside. It was very late. He didn't want to wake anyone—especially his mean mother-in-law, Pearl. She was visiting for only a few days. But already she was making Fred miserable. For some reason, Pearl had never liked Fred. And waking her up wouldn't make her like him any more.

Once again, Dino made a mad rush for Fred. This time, Fred was ready. He tossed Dino a dinosaur biscuit. Munch, munch. Dino was too busy chewing to make his usual charge.

Whew! Fred was safe. Carefully, he took another step—right onto a toy car. The car rolled forward. And Fred flew up into the air. Boom! He landed flat on his back, his bowling trophy at his side. The whole house shook with the force.

Pearl came running. Even in the middle of the night, she was wearing her furs and jewels.

"Look at you!" she cried. "What a fat oaf!"

Wilma was right behind her mother. She helped Fred to his feet, while he glared at Pearl. This was *his* home!

"Why, I've got half a mind—" he growled.

"Half a mind? Don't flatter yourself," Pearl shot back.

"Stop it. Both of you," Wilma pleaded, trying to keep the peace. "Fred is a loving husband and a good provider."

"Oh?" said Pearl. "What has he ever provided you with besides shade? You could have married Elliot Bridgestone, the man who invented the wheel. Instead, you picked Fred Flintstone. The man who invented the excuse!"

Was that true? Fred wondered. Was he a failure? No! he decided. He couldn't be!

"I'm not going to be a nobody my whole life," he

announced to Pearl. "One day I'm going to be a somebody. We'll live in the lap of luxury. Wilma will have everything she deserves."

Pearl sniffed the air, and turned on her heel. She didn't believe a word he said.

I'll show her, Fred thought. I'll show everybody!

CHAPTER 4

The next day, same as always, Fred went to his job at the quarry. And, same as always, he and Barney ate lunch together.

Fred munched on a three-foot prehistoric drumstick. Barney had his usual giant hard-boiled dinosaur egg. He was just about to dig in, when Cliff Vandercave came to the lunch area.

What was a bigwig doing down in the quarry? Everyone but Fred stopped eating.

"Gentlemen," Cliff said. "I have an important announcement. There is a new program here at Slate and Co. Construction. We call it the Executive Placement Program. An aptitude test will be given on Saturday. And whoever scores the highest will be our new vice president"—Cliff paused for a moment. He wanted everyone's complete attention— "with a big salary and a shiny new nameplate."

A shiny new nameplate! Fred stopped eating. This was his chance to be somebody!

All week long, Fred studied and studied for the aptitude test. He didn't go bowling. He didn't go to lodge meetings. All he did was read, write, multiply, and divide. Fred was determined to get the highest score.

Finally, it was Saturday. Fred was so nervous, Barney drove him to the quarry. But when they got to the testing area, Fred only felt worse. There were so many workers taking the test. Men. Apes. Neanderthals. How could he compete?

"Let's get out of here, Barney," he said in a low voice. "I'm not the executive type."

"Look, Fred. If it makes you feel any better, I'll take the test too," Barney said, leading him to a desk. That helped. Fred actually smiled at his friend.

Then Cliff Vandercave cleared his throat. "Please take your seats," he said. "You will have one hour to complete the exam. Carve all answers with a well-sharpened number two chisel."

Fred and Barney settled into their seats. Each desk had a stone tablet on it.

"Begin!" said Cliff.

Fred looked at his tablet. Oh no! There were so many questions! The answers—what were the answers? He thought and thought and thought some more—all about question number one. Finally he chiseled in his answer. But was it right? He erased it. Then he put in a different answer. A second later, he erased that one, too. Fred wasn't sure about anything!

Seconds turned into minutes, and the minutes turned into an hour.

"Chisels down!" called Cliff, checking his hour-glass watch. "Please slide your answer slab into the envelope provided. Then bring everything to the front."

Fred wiped the sweat from his brow. He smiled feebly. He didn't want anyone to know how badly he'd done.

But Barney knew Fred better than anyone.

"Here. Let me take that up for you," he said to Fred, reaching for his envelope.

On the way to the front, Barney stole a look at Fred's answer tablet. It was a mess. "Oh boy," said Barney. "He even left the 'e' off Flintstone."

Suddenly Barney remembered the toast he'd made to Fred. *I stand before my peers and vow I'll pay him back someday, somehow.*

Making sure no one noticed, Barney switched tests with Fred. This could be the way, he thought.

Cliff brought the tests up to his office for Miss Stone to grade. A little later, she was finished.

"Believe it or not, the high scorer was Fred Flintstone!"

"Flintstone!" said Cliff in surprise. "That can't be right. He's dense. He's stupid."

"He's perfect," Miss Stone put in.

Cliff bared his teeth in an oily grin. Miss Stone was right. Fred Flintstone was so stupid, he would play right into their hands. He hurried down to the quarry and called all the workers together.

For a moment, Fred stood quietly with the others. But he couldn't bear to hear the bad news. He'd studied so hard—and for nothing!

"Come on, Barn," he said to his friend. "Let's go. This is a waste of time."

"Our new executive is—" Cliff was saying.

Fred turned to leave.

"—Mr. Fred Flintstone!"

"What'd I tell you," Fred said, still walking away. "Waste of—" Then he stopped in his tracks. "Quick, Barney! What's my name?"

"Fred Flintstone," Barney said, laughing. "With

an 'e'. Fred, it's you! You made it!"

Fred jumped two feet in the air. "YABBA-DABBA-DOO!" he cried. Finally! He was some-body! Barney grinned at his best friend. He couldn't have been happier.

CHAPTER 5

Fred was set to begin his new job right away. On Monday morning, he put on a brand-new zebra-striped suit. Then he slicked back his hair.

"How do I look?" he asked Pebbles.

"Daddy pretty," she said. Fred was feeling pretty—pretty good! He kissed Wilma good-bye and hurried out the door. He didn't want to be late.

A little while later, he and Barney were driving to work. "So, Fred," Barney said in a teasing voice. "What do I call you now? Mr. Flintstone? Boss? Sir?"

"Nah," said Fred, laughing. "A simple Your Highness will do." Then Fred turned serious. "I'm not going to be one of those guys who makes it to the top and forgets where he came from. I'm going to get everyone in the quarry some vacation time."

"You know what I really wish you could get for us?" said Barney. "Those little packets of ketchup in the lunchroom."

"Hey! I'm just one man," Fred told him with a smile.

"Not from the back," chuckled Barney as he got out of the car. They were at the quarry.

"Well, I guess this is it." He straightened Fred's tie for him. Then the two friends headed in different directions. Barney to the dirty, dusty quarry. And Fred to the shiny, clean executive building.

"Hey Barney?" Fred called out.

"Yeah, Fred?" Barney thought Fred was going to say something sentimental. Something about already missing his days in the quarry.

"Can you spot me a few sand dollars? I'm short this week." Barney smiled as he reached into his pocket. Some things never changed. Pocketing the money, Fred went inside the building without looking back.

The busy lobby was filled with men in suits. People were rushing everywhere. Fred gawked at each passerby as he made his way upstairs. Cliff was waiting.

"Welcome aboard, Flintstone," he said. "It's good to have you here. Any gravel-brain can shovel rock. But up here it's different. We're different."

Cliff led Fred to his office door. There was Fred's shiny new nameplate, and inside was the most incredible room Fred had ever seen.

"Wow!" said Fred. "This is mine? My office? My desk? My chair?"

"Yes, yes, yes," replied Cliff, wishing Fred would just go inside.

Finally, Fred walked in. On the far wall, a big picture window overlooked the quarry. Fred could see all his buddies hard at work. Next to the desk was a dignified-looking bird. Nice touch, thought Fred. An office pet.

Suddenly, a smooth female voice interrupted his thoughts. "Is this a good time?"

"I'd like you to meet Miss Stone," Cliff said to Fred. "She's your new secretary." This was too much! A desk, a chair, *and* a gorgeous secretary!

"How would you like your coffee?" Miss Stone asked, smiling at Fred.

She was so pretty, Fred had trouble thinking straight. "Um . . . in a cup?" he sputtered out.

Miss Stone nodded her head. "Bold choice," she said approvingly.

Cliff and Miss Stone exchanged looks as they left the office together. So far, so good. They *wanted*

Fred to think he was bold. Smart. In charge. It was all part of the plan.

Now that he was alone, Fred sat down in his chair. He put his feet up on the desk and leaned way back. This was going to be a piece of cake.

"Take a memo," he said, practicing what he would say to Miss Stone. "To Cliff Vandercave: Let's play golf."

Fred leaned back a little more. "Executively yours, Fred Fliiiiiiaaaah!" he cried, flipping over.

"Are there six or seven *i's* in 'iiiiiiaaaah'?" said a voice.

"Who said that?" Fred peered over his desk. There was nobody in the room.

"It was I. Your Dictabird."

The bird had spoken? Fred stood up for a closer look.

"To Cliff Vandercave: Let's play golf," the bird said. He was imitating Fred perfectly. At last Fred understood. The bird wasn't a pet after all. He was a tape recorder.

"Mr. Flintstone," the bird continued in his own voice. "I'd like to warn you. You are in a dangerous situation here. But whenever you're confused, you can come to me."

"Oh really?" Fred said. "Look, Birdie. Let's get

the pecking order straight here. I don't need any help from you. I'm vice president!"

Fred went to the window and shouted, "I'm vice president!" The quarry workers looked up and cheered for their old buddy.

So there, thought Fred.

Cliff was shooting baskets in his office. Miss Stone was busy working, chiseling some forms at his desk.

"There," she said. "I'm finished. What do you think of these documents?"

Cliff looked them over. "Perfect. They look just like the real ones. Mr. Flintstone is about to steal a great deal of money from Mr. Slate. Too bad *we* get to keep it."

"We can get him to sign these right away," Miss Stone said, getting up from her chair.

"No." Cliff was thinking things over carefully. "First we have to make sure he'll do anything we say."

Back in his office, Fred was playing with the Dictabird.

"Fred is the greatest bowler on earth," he said.

"Fred is the greatest bowler on earth," the Dictabird repeated.

Cliff listened to the exchange from the hallway.

This is going to be easy! he thought, walking in.

"I have an assignment for you," he told Fred. "Are you ready for your first executive action?"

Fred looked up from his empty desk and smiled. Finally, a chance to prove himself! "Ready and willing. Whatever you need, consider it done."

"Good," Cliff said. "Your job . . . is to fire Bernard Rubble."

CHAPTER 6

"Come on, Fred," Barney said. They were driving home from work. "Usually you yak my ear off. But you haven't said two words. Something exciting must have happened today."

Fred was too upset to talk. Fire Barney? His best friend? Just when he and Betty adopted a son? Just when they needed the money most? And why did Fred have to fire him? Because he got the lowest score on the aptitude test! Brains weren't everything, Fred thought. After all, not everyone could be as smart as he was.

But still . . . Fred knew if he didn't fire Barney, somebody else would. Somebody Barney didn't even know.

Fred put his heel to the ground and stopped the car. They were home.

"Mind if I come in for a minute?" Barney asked as they got out of the car.

"Sure," said Fred. "There's something I want to talk to you about." Fred opened the door to his house.

"Surprise!"

It was a surprise party! Fred's buddies from the quarry were there. So were his lodge brothers. Even his mother-in-law Pearl had come to congratulate Fred.

"This is all Betty and Barney's doing," Wilma told Fred. "They wanted to celebrate your new job. Aren't we lucky to have friends like them?"

What could Fred say? He felt terrible. And it didn't help when Pearl came rushing over. "There's my big, handsome son-in-law," she said, giving him a hug. "I knew this day would come. I always told Wilma to hang onto you. Have you lost weight?"

Fred looked Pearl up and down. "Have we met?" he asked. But Pearl just laughed, and hugged him even harder.

Then Barney called for everyone's attention. "Fred, Betty and I got you a little something," he announced. "Something to show you how proud we are."

Betty held out a shiny new briefcase with a bow on it.

"Ooh. Ahh!" everyone exclaimed. Now Fred felt even worse. He couldn't take a gift from somebody he was firing!

"I can't accept this," he said.

"Fred, take it. It's yours," said Barney.

"No. It's not."

"Yes, it is," said Betty.

"Take a hint, Shorty." Now Pearl was on the scene. "My Freddie doesn't want that tacky thing."

Barney couldn't understand. He'd paid top dollar for it. "Why don't you want it?"

"Because," Fred said with a sigh, "you can't afford it, pal. You're fired."

Fred took Barney out to the patio. Tears streamed down Fred's face. Barney patted his arm, trying to comfort him.

"Come on, Fred," he said. "You didn't have a choice."

"No. A man always has a choice. I'll quit tomorrow." Fred looked at Barney hopefully. Maybe he would talk him out of it.

"Well, if you want to quit . . . " Barney said.

"Now don't say anything to change my mind," Fred interrupted. He sighed. "If only this job didn't mean so much to Wilma."

"Fred—" Barney began to say more.

"All right," Fred put in before Barney could continue. "If you feel that strongly about it, I won't quit. Happy now?" He pretended to be angry.

"Thanks, Fred. I appreciate it," Barney told him. "But I have to ask you a question. Why are they canning me?"

A pitying look crossed Fred's face. "Barney, you're a wonderful father. A loving husband. A good bowler. But none of that counts on an aptitude test. You had the lowest score, Barn."

The lowest score! Slowly, the news sank in. Barney had switched tests to help Fred. He was glad to do it, too. But now it had cost him his job!

CHAPTER 7

Two weeks went by. Each morning, Barney would leave home, looking for work. But jobs were hard to come by. Barney was getting worried.

Each morning Fred would leave his house, too. But Fred was going to work, with his shiny new briefcase in hand. He didn't have a care in the world. Fred would walk through the lobby with his head held high. He was a vice president.

One morning, an executive meeting was being held in the boardroom. Of course, being an executive, Fred had to be there. He walked into the room. A dozen bigwigs—all with slicked-back hair and fancy suits—frowned. But Fred didn't notice a thing.

"Sorry I'm late," he said cheerfully, taking a seat. "I had a little car trouble. I picked up a nail."

Fred held his foot up, to show everyone the bandage.

"Thank you, Mr. Flagstone," Mr. Slate said coldly. He always got Fred's name wrong. Then he turned to Cliff. "May we continue?"

Cliff snapped his fingers, and a large-scale model was lowered from the ceiling. It was a model of the quarry. But the quarry looked different. It looked almost . . . modern.

"We can revolutionize the building industry," Cliff announced. "We can make simple, cheap housing units with this new equipment."

Then Cliff explained: Steam-powered conveyor belts—not quarry workers—would carry boulders to a rock-slicing machine. There, the boulders would be cut and shaped into walls and roofs.

"The customers will love it," Cliff told everyone. "And we'll make four times the profit!"

Everyone oohed and ahhed.

"Very impressive," said Mr. Slate. "We should build this system right away."

Fred stood up. Something was bothering him.

"I know I'm the new man here," Fred said with a modest smile. "But I don't think you hired me to look pretty."

That got everyone's attention.

"Now I know from up here that quarry looks

small. But I've spent a lot of time down there. And let me tell you, those are BIG rocks." Fred waved at the model. "And there's no way this little doo-dad is going to do the job." He turned to Cliff. "Sorry to burst your bubble," he said graciously.

For a moment, there was silence. The executives were too shocked to speak. Was somebody standing up to Cliff Vandercave?

Then Cliff began to laugh. "What a comedian," he said. "Mr. Slate, we've found a host for our company talent show."

Mr. Slate laughed too. And pretty soon *everyone* was laughing.

Fred didn't know what was going on. But just to be safe, he threw in a few guffaws. Maybe it was better to go along with the crowd just this once. . . .

Later that day, Fred was in his office, dictating a memo to the Dictabird.

"In conclusion, Mr. Slate, I feel a paid vacation is in order for everyone at the quarry." Fred meant to stand by his promises to Barney. But he didn't get any further. Miss Stone came in with a stack of forms.

"Here are today's requisitions," she told Fred.

"They're all ready for your signature."

"You know," Fred said, "I've been signing these forms for weeks now. I hate to pry, but what are they?"

"Oh, just some silly little forms so we can pay the men for the modernization." Miss Stone gave Fred a dazzling smile. And just like that, Fred forgot all about those silly little forms. He smiled back. He was so busy smiling, he didn't even notice Wilma standing by the door.

"Ahem!" the Dictabird said, trying to get Fred's attention.

Finally Fred looked up. "Wilma! What a surprise!" He introduced Wilma to Miss Stone. But Miss Stone was already leaving the office, patting Pebbles on the head as she left.

"Your secretary is very pretty," Wilma said, looking after her.

"Really? I hadn't noticed. Hey, Wilma! Have you ever seen one of these Dictabirds?" Fred was trying to change the subject.

He turned to the Dictabird and said, "My wife is the most beautiful gal in Bedrock."

"My wife is the most beautiful gal in Bedrock," the Dictabird repeated. He sounded just like Fred. But Wilma wasn't paying attention. She had one thing on her mind. It wasn't the Dictabird. It wasn't Miss Stone. It was the Rubbles.

"Betty and Barney don't have any money left," she told Fred. "They have to rent out their house to make ends meet. So they're moving in with us!"

CHAPTER 8

Wilma and Fred planned a special dinner to welcome the Rubbles to their home. Fred was barbecuing bronto steaks on the grill.

"How about this?" he said to Barney. "The Flintstones and the Rubbles under one roof!" Suddenly, Dino grabbed a steak and took off.

"Hey, Barn," Fred called out. "You like yours rare, right?"

"Yeah," said Barney.

"Well then, that one's yours!" Barney raced after Dino, trying to get back his dinner.

Inside, Wilma and Betty were making a salad. Betty chopped the lettuce. Wilma sliced the cucumber. But she was also keeping one eye on Betty.

Wilma frowned. Betty should tear the lettuce,

not chop it. She didn't want to criticize, but she couldn't help herself.

"It's really better if you tear the lettuce instead of hacking it with a knife."

Betty suggested they switch jobs. Now Betty was slicing the cucumber. But Wilma didn't think she was doing that quite right either. They just could not agree.

Even Pebbles wasn't happy. She didn't want to share her stone-age toys. "Mine!" she said to Bamm-Bamm.

The Flintstones and the Rubbles were *not* getting along.

A few days later, Fred sat in the boardroom eating his lunch. He was thinking about all those other lunches—lunches with his buddies down in the quarry. Fred hated to admit it, but he missed those days.

Now he ate alone, each and every day. It was enough to make him lose his appetite. Well, almost enough, Fred thought. He polished off his sandwich in two big bites.

What should he do now? Fred wandered over to the model of the new quarry. He picked up a boulder, and loaded it onto the catapult. Zing! The boulder flew onto the conveyor belt. Then the conveyor belt took the boulder straight to the rock-slicing machine. A perfect shot.

Fred put another boulder into place. "Flintstone has the rock," he said, speaking like a sportscaster. "He lines up his shot. He shoots. . . . Oops!"

The boulder crashed into the rock-slicing machine. Miss Stone walked in, just in time to see the machine fall apart.

"I'll get someone to fix that," she told Fred.

"Wait a minute," Fred said. "Can I ask you something?"

Miss Stone nodded.

"I can't understand all this stuff." Fred waved at the fancy machinery. "But wouldn't this put a lot of my buddies out of work?"

Miss Stone looked closely at Fred. He cared about people. That was obvious. And Miss Stone remembered how sweet he was with Wilma. She was beginning to respect him.

In the meantime though, there was Cliff's scheme to worry about. Miss Stone decided to go to Cliff and speak her mind. She hurried to his office.

"I'm worried," she told Cliff. "Fred . . . uh, Mr. Flintstone . . . is smarter than we thought. Maybe we should quit while we're ahead."

Cliff was shaving in his office. He put his rodent razor down for a moment. The little rodent shut his mouth, giving his teeth a rest.

"I've got a better idea. If Mr. Flintstone is such a hard worker, we'll give him something to take his mind off work."

A few minutes later, he dumped a bagful of sand dollars on Fred's desk.

"A bonus?" said Fred. "For me?" He couldn't believe it.

"That's right, Flintstone. You deserve it. And just between us . . . if you want to be a top executive here, you have to start living like one."

CHAPTER 9

Fred had so many sand dollars now, he didn't know what to do. At last, he could give Wilma everything she deserved. But what should he buy? Fred decided to start out small. He bought a new Pigasaurus garbage disposal. Then he bought a new car with the license plate YABADO. Then he took Wilma shopping.

At first, Wilma didn't want the pearls, the dresses, the hats. But everything was so lovely. How could she resist?

Soon the Flintstones had all new clothes . . . all new furniture . . . a brand-new boat . . . an addition to the house . . . even a pool for their backyard.

"Who said money doesn't buy happiness?" Fred said, lazily swimming a lap.

Wilma looked at all their new belongings. Her eyes stopped on Dino's diamond-studded collar. "But Fred, isn't this too much too fast?"

Fred stopped swimming. "In the buffet of life," he told Wilma, "there are no second helpings. You've got to fill your plate."

Betty and Barney were watching from inside. Betty stood over the sink, doing the dishes. Again. And Barney had just finished mowing the lawn. Again. While Fred and Wilma were enjoying all their latest luxuries, Betty and Barney had been keeping their home in order.

Betty wiped her hands and turned to her husband. "They've changed, Barney. I hardly know them since Fred became such a big shot."

Barney sighed. He could have been the one spending all those sand dollars without a care in the world. Instead, he wound up out of work. If only . . .

"Ah, come on," Barney told himself. "It's all sour grapes. Get over it already!"

A few days later, Fred was getting ready to leave work when Cliff came into his office. He had more forms for Fred to sign.

"What are they?" Fred asked.

"Just sign these and all your buddies down in

the quarry will get some time off."

Fred smiled. "Mr. Slate finally noticed my memos! I hope the guys will know I'm the one to thank!"

Cliff smiled his nasty grin. "Don't worry, Flintstone," he said as he was leaving. "You'll get all the credit."

Fred picked up his chisel. He was ready to chip in his name. But the Dictabird stopped him.

"Mr. Flintstone," said the bird, walking over to stand on the documents. "Up to now our relationship has not been . . ." He trailed off, trying to find a word Fred would understand. "I'll put it simply for you. You hate my bird guts. But I feel a sense of loyalty to you. Listen to this piece of advice: Only an idiot signs something before he reads it."

Fred was enraged. The nerve of that bird!

"I'm the executive," he shouted. "You're the office equipment! And if I were going to ask office equipment for advice, I'd go to the watercooler."

He pulled the tablet away from the Dictabird, and left in a huff.

After all, he thought, he was the big cheese here. Not that stupid bird. Tonight he was taking his wife to Cavern on the Green, the fanciest restaurant in town. He didn't see the Dictabird going anywhere!

Fred drove by his house to pick up Wilma and Betty. Barney was going to meet them later.

"Barney started a new job today," Betty explained. "I don't know what time he'll get off."

Inside the restaurant, elegantly dressed men and women dined at candlelit tables. A live band played the latest hits. Fred, Wilma, and Betty took their seats. Then a busboy came over to fill their water glasses.

Betty glanced at the busboy. Then she looked again. "Barney?" Barney was working at Cavern on the Green!

Wilma and Betty were embarrassed. It was strange being waited on by Barney. But Fred was glad.

"See, Wilma? And you were afraid he'd never find a job. You thought we'd be stuck with them for— ouch!" Wilma had kicked Fred under the table.

Meanwhile, Barney had to get back to work. He went into the kitchen to get more glasses. Inside, the cooks were watching CNN, Cave News Network, on TV. Something on the screen caught Barney's eye.

"Quarry workers are demonstrating," a reporter was saying. "They are protesting the layoff of the entire labor force."

In the background, Barney saw workers carrying signs. One sign read: FLINTSTONE SOLD US OUT!

Barney rushed back to the table. "Hey, Fred, do you know what happened to everyone at the quarry today?"

"Well, I oughtta," Fred boasted. "It was my idea. A few hours ago, I sent them off on a nice long vacation."

Barney was steaming. "You mean a permanent vacation. You fired them!"

"Fred! How could you?" Wilma said, shocked.

"But I didn't," said Fred.

"Yes, you did," Barney put in. "It's all over the news!"

Wilma was confused. What really happened?

"Come on, Wilma!" Fred was pleading with her. "Who are you going to believe—me or some busboy?"

Now Betty spoke up. "That busboy is your best friend!"

"Best friend?" said Fred. "I lost my best friend the day I became vice president. He's jealous of my hard-earned success."

Hard-earned? That did it. Barney couldn't keep quiet anymore. "You only got that job because I switched tests with you!" he burst out.

"Finally," Betty said to Wilma. "This all makes sense."

"You *don't* belive this!" said Wilma.

"Are you calling my husband a liar?"

"After all we've done for you!"

"Rich snobs!"

"Ingrates!"

"Come on, Barney," Betty said, leading her husband out of the restaurant. They were both so angry, they didn't care if Barney lost his job. "We're moving out tonight!"

CHAPTER 10

When Wilma and Fred got home from the restaurant, the Rubbles were almost ready to leave.

Fred went straight to his Bark-o'-Lounger chair, ignoring everyone. He didn't say a word. He just held his news slab in front of his face. But Wilma rushed around after Betty, trying to get her to stop packing.

"Come on, Betty," Wilma said. "We all said things we didn't mean." How could the Rubbles move out? she thought. Where would they go? What would they do? And what would Wilma do without her best friend?

But it was too late to patch things up.

"Good-bye, Wilma," Betty said, giving her a quick hug. A second later, Betty, Barney, and

Bamm-Bamm were out the door, with Bamm-Bamm carrying all their belongings on his back. Pebbles waved to him sadly.

Finally, Fred put down his news slab. "At last!" he said. "Now I can walk around in my underwear again."

"That's more important than twenty years of friendship?" Wilma asked tearfully.

"It is on a hot day. We'll make new friends, Wilma. There are four thousand other people in this world. Who needs the Rubbles?"

"I do! But I don't need this necklace." Wilma ripped off her new pearl necklace and threw it on the floor. "Or this bracelet. Or these drapes. . . ." Wilma was on a rampage, throwing everything on the ground.

"No, Wilma! Not the TV!" Fred shouted.

But the new wide-screen set was already broken to bits.

"I don't care about any of this stuff," Wilma said. "And I don't care for what we've become." She packed some clothes in an old suitcase. A few minutes later she left the house, taking Pebbles and Dino with her.

Fred stood at the door. "All right, Wilma," he shouted after her. "Come back now and I'll forgive you." Then he whispered, "Please?"

But Wilma was already gone.

Wilma and Pebbles were staying at Pearl's house for a while. And the Rubbles were camping out, pretending they enjoyed the fresh air. Fred had never felt so alone in his life. Still, he decided to act as if nothing had changed. He'd go to work like nothing was wrong.

The next morning, Fred drove up to the quarry gates. The demonstration was still going on. Workers carried signs and shouted, "Fred is dead!"

Then his old buddies caught sight of him. They rushed over. "You're a traitor, Flintstone!" one cried out.

"And you're a rotten bowler, too!" another shouted.

"Listen to me!" Fred said, trying to explain. "I'm your friend."

But the workers didn't listen. They just threw stale old vegetables. Security guards had to help Fred into the office building.

When he was safely inside, Fred straightened his shoulders. This was all a mistake. And he was going to get to the bottom of it. Fred strode through the lobby, into the elevator, and right into the file room. He opened up all the drawers.

"That should do it!" he said, taking out all the

forms he signed. Then he hurried to his office. It took him a while. But Fred carefully read through everything.

"I can't believe it!" he finally shouted, slamming down the last document. It shattered into bits. "They've made a fool out of me."

"Yes, but look what they had to work with!" the Dictabird said back.

Just then Cliff and Miss Stone came into Fred's office.

"Find anything interesting?" Cliff asked with a sneer.

"Yeah. I'm onto your little scam. You've been billing phony companies—and keeping the money for yourself. I'm going to Mr. Slate!"

"Sure," said Cliff. "But remember, you'll get all the credit. It's your signature on those forms."

"I never touched that money!" Fred protested.

"Oh, please. You redid your house. Bought a car. Jewelry."

"I'm innocent," cried Fred.

"Oh, boo-hoo." Cliff turned to Miss Stone. "Call security. Tell them we've found a crook."

Miss Stone hesitated. Then she walked over to the phone, passing close by Fred. "Run while you have the chance," she whispered.

CHAPTER 11

Now, Fred was on the lam. From the police. From the quarry workers. From everyone!

Back at the Flintstones' house, Wilma heard a soft knock at the door. Could it be Fred? She was so worried about him. And she missed him, too. Pearl was back to hating him. But Wilma still loved her husband—no matter what.

Wilma opened the door. It was Betty and Bamm-Bamm.

"I don't care what Barney says," Betty told her friend. "I couldn't let you go through this alone."

"Bamm-Bamm!" said Pebbles. She toddled to her friend, and everyone hugged.

Then Wilma turned on the TV. It was time for "Bedrock's Most Wanted." Fred's face filled the screen. "We now bring you a dramatization of the story that's rocked our city," said the host.

A room set up to look like Fred's office appeared on the screen. Then TV actors portraying Fred, Cliff, and Miss Stone walked in.

"How could you marry that man?" Pearl demanded. She pointed to "Fred," who was stuffing money into his briefcase.

"Mother! That's not my husband. That's an actor! Anyway, Fred might be a lot of things. But a thief isn't one of them."

"Can you prove it?" asked Pearl.

Wilma wanted to. More than anything in the world. But how? Then she noticed something on TV—something in Fred's office. And she knew what she had to do.

Wilma and Betty asked Pearl to baby-sit Pebbles and Bamm-Bamm. Then they took Pearl's car, and sped straight to Fred's office.

Betty and Wilma snuck quietly inside the building. When they came back out, Wilma was clutching the Dictabird. The bird knew everything that went on in the office. He could tell the police the truth—word for word. Fred would be cleared!

Wilma didn't know it, but Cliff and Miss Stone were in the building too. They were at the safe, packing the stolen sand dollars into satchels. They were almost ready to leave town with all the money.

Cliff paused for a moment. He wasn't used to actually working. And he needed a break. While Miss Stone packed, Cliff strolled over to the window. He looked down—just as Wilma and Betty raced back to the car. Cliff was surprised. "What would Flintstone's wife want with that stinky Dicta—" Then it hit him.

She must be stopped.

Meanwhile, Fred was in big trouble. An angry mob had found him. Now they were chasing him through the streets. Fred turned a corner, hoping to find a way to escape. Instead, a second angry mob came racing toward him.

Fred had nowhere to run. Nowhere to hide. He was surrounded. There was nothing to do but plead.

"Wait!" he shouted. "You can't do this. I was framed!"

The mob pressed in even closer. The pleading wasn't working.

Just then a strange light settled on the crowd. Soft music began to play. It was an ice-cream truck, making the neighborhood rounds.

"Anybody want a sno-cone?" asked the driver.

"Barney!" said Fred.

Fred was always glad to see the ice-cream man. But now, the timing couldn't have been better. He forgot his pride. He forgot to be stubborn. He only remembered Barney was his friend. "Am I glad to see you!"

"You know him?" one man asked Barney.

"Yeah," said Barney. "He used to be my best friend. And I guess in a way, I'm responsible for this whole mess."

That's all the mob had to hear. They grabbed Barney, too.

"Did you come here to save me?" Fred asked above their shouts.

"Save you? I saw a crowd. I figured I could sell a few sno-cones."

Fred's heart sank. Barney hadn't forgiven him after all. "Look, Barney," he said. "I know you're a little mad at me right now." He looked nervously at the crowd. "But you're the best friend a guy ever had. And me? I'm nothing but a big jerk."

Barney sighed. How could he stay mad after a speech like that? Fred and Barney went to hug. But by now, their hands were tied. They could only shake pinkies.

"Let's get them!" said someone in the crowd.

This is it, thought Fred. He squeezed his eyes

shut. He didn't want to watch. Suddenly, he heard the squeal of tires, and someone shouting.

"Wait! Stop! Fred's innocent!" It was Wilma and Betty!

The mob parted to let them through. Wilma showed everyone the Dictabird. "Go ahead," she told the bird. "Tell them the whole story." The Dictabird closed his mouth tight.

"Please," said Wilma.

Finally the bird said, "All right. But I would like an apology first."

"Okay, I'm sorry," said Barney.

"Not you. Him." The Dictabird nodded his head at Fred. "You treated me badly, Mr. Flintstone. And you hurt my feelings. Even a bird has feelings."

Well . . . Fred guessed he could have been a little nicer. A little more sensitive.

"I'm sorry," he mumbled.

"Thank you, sir," the Dictabird said. He ruffled his feathers importantly. "Now gather around, everyone. And I'll tell you a tale. . . ."

A little while later, Fred and Wilma and Barney and Betty were on their way back to the Flintstones'. Everything's going to be fine, thought Fred. Wilma was not mad anymore. He and Barney were friends again. People knew the truth about the money.

Fred drove faster. He couldn't wait to see Pebbles. She'd run to the door like she always did, whenever he came home.

But when he opened the door, Pebbles didn't come running. No one did. The house was in shambles. Furniture was turned over. Drawers were opened. Clothes were strewn everywhere.

"What happened?" said Barney. Wilma and Betty were right behind him.

"Pebbles!" cried Wilma.

"Bamm-Bamm!" Betty shouted.

They hurried to the nursery.

Then Fred saw Dino and Pearl. They were lying on the floor—tied up and gagged! Fred rushed over to Pearl. And he stepped right over her to untie Dino.

Wilma and Betty came running back into the room. "Pebbles and Bamm-Bamm are gone!" Wilma shouted.

"This was in the crib," said Betty, handing a note slab to Fred. He read it aloud.

"If you want to see your kids again, bring the Dictabird to the quarry at dawn. No police."

Fred squeezed the stone note until it turned to dust.

CHAPTER 12

The sun was just coming up over Bedrock. It was dawn. Outside the rock quarry, Fred squared his shoulders. It was time for action. Together, he and Barney walked through the gates. Fred held the Dictabird in his arms. He was scared and angry and nervous. But more than anything, he was determined.

Up ahead, Fred saw the new quarry equipment. Everything was in place. The catapult. The rock-slicing machine. The conveyor belt.

The conveyor belt! Fred gasped. Pebbles and Bamm-Bamm were strapped tightly onto the belt. And Cliff Vandercave was standing right next to the giant on/off switch. Big boulders sat on the conveyor belt in front of the kids. The catapult was poised, ready to shoot more boulders behind them.

"Bamm-Bamm!" said Barney. He started toward his son.

"First hand over that bird," ordered Cliff.

"Don't worry," Fred whispered to the Dictabird, and put him on the ground. The bird looked at Fred and nodded. Then he made his way across the quarry yard.

"Thank you, gentlemen," Cliff said, scooping up the bird. He started to leave. But he turned back. He flipped the switch to "on." Then he ran.

The machinery began to rumble. The catapult shot a boulder into the air. The conveyor belt gave a jerk. It started to move!

One boulder dropped into the rock-slicing machine. Then another. Pebbles and Bamm-Bamm were moving along the conveyor belt. They were getting closer to the slicer!

Fred and Barney ran for the switch. They tried to turn it off. But the switch was stuck. It wouldn't budge.

"You keep trying to shut it off," Barney told Fred. "I'll get the kids!"

Fred kept pulling. He pulled so hard, the lever broke right off. Fred gave it a kick. He knew the machinery was cheap—the money for better equipment had gone right into Cliff's pockets.

Barney jumped into the catapult. The next

instant, he was shot up into the air—over the conveyor belt, and smack into a wall.

"Owww!" he yelled, sliding down next to Pebbles and Bamm-Bamm. He was out cold.

Meanwhile, the Dictabird was trying to escape. He bit Cliff's hand. "Hey!" Cliff shouted, dropping the bird. Panting with every step he took, the bird raced back to Fred. But he wasn't safe yet. Cliff was right behind him.

Fred didn't notice. He was too busy studying the machine. Fred had to think of something—and quick. Then he remembered what happened in the boardroom. How the misfired boulder destroyed the quarry model. Fred just had to move the catapult, so the next boulder would crash into the rock slicer.

Putting his shoulder to the catapult, Fred pushed. Every muscle in his body strained with the effort. But the catapult was too heavy. It didn't move. Then Fred thought of Pebbles in danger, and suddenly he had the strength of ten men. He pushed again. Finally, the catapult groaned. A second later, it shifted.

"There!" said Fred. The catapult was aimed right at the rock-slicing machine.

Just then the Dictabird ran between Fred's legs. "Save me!" he cried. "I have a wife and three eggs!"

Cliff was closing in fast. And in his hand, he held a slingshot with a sharp rock in it. "Kiss your bird good-bye!" he said.

Cliff raised his weapon. He was just about to fire. But a satchel filled with sand dollars came down on his head.

"Will there be anything else, Mr. Flintstone?" asked Miss Stone, holding the satchel. During those last few hours, Miss Stone had done a lot of thinking. And she had decided to do the right thing. She had come to Fred's rescue.

"Hold my calls," said Fred. He made sure the catapult was in place. Then, with Miss Stone and the Dictabird cheering him on, he fired the next boulder.

The boulder went flying . . . up . . . up . . . up. It was a direct hit! Gears and nuts and bolts and springs went flying. Steam hissed out of the machine. It was going crazy. Instead of slicing the rocks, it was crushing them!

Just that minute, Barney came to. Quickly, he grabbed the kids and jumped off the conveyor belt to safety.

"Yabba-dabba-doo!" shouted Fred, running over to hug his daughter.

Now water and bits of rock were spewing out of

the machine, and flowing downhill through the quarry. It was like a river.

"Come on," said Fred, herding everyone to safety.

Then Fred noticed Cliff. He was rubbing his head, and getting awkwardly to his feet. He was going to make a run for it! Grabbing the sand dollars, Cliff took off, scrambling down the hill toward his car.

"Not so fast," said Fred, picking up a nice round boulder. He held it like a bowling ball. Then he stood up on his tiptoes, took a few steps forward, and let the ball go.

Fred twisted right and the ball went right. He twisted left and ball went left. Boom! It knocked Cliff right over.

"Steeee-rike!" cried Fred.

Cliff wasn't down for long. He stood back up. But there was a strange whooshing noise coming from above. The rock and water river was flowing right above him. A second later, it came rushing down, covering him from head to toe. Cliff was frozen in his tracks—just like a statue.

Then, all of a sudden, police cars roared up to the scene. Wilma and Betty had led them to the quarry, with Mr. Slate right behind.

The Dictabird gave the police his statement. Fred was a free man, once again. But the police had to arrest Miss Stone.

"Oh, Mr. Flintstone," she said with a small smile. "I may not be in on Monday."

"Don't worry, Miss Stone," Fred told her. "I'll make sure they let you off easy."

Fred glanced at Mr. Slate. He wasn't sure his boss would let *him* off easy. The quarry was a mess. And all the new equipment was still going haywire—thanks to Fred Flintstone.

"Flintstone!" Mr. Slate was calling him over. Fred sighed. Of course Mr. Slate got his name right now.

"How did this happen?" he asked Fred, pointing to the statuelike Cliff.

"Well, the equipment went crazy. The rocks got crushed. And they got mixed up with water. Then it all fell down the hill. I'm real sorry."

"Sorry?" said Mr. Slate. "I love this rock and water stuff. I'm going to name it after my daughter, Concretia. And thanks to concrete, the Stone Age is over. Now Flintstone, I want you to hire back all the men. We are going into production. Immediately!"

"We?" said Fred.

"Of course! You are hereby promoted to president of the Concrete Division!"

Fred started to cheer. "Yabba-dabba—" But he stopped before he got to "doo." Fred knew he deserved the job this time. But that didn't change the way he felt.

"I have to turn you down," he told Mr. Slate. "You see, all my life I wanted to be a somebody. And when I finally was, I became somebody I didn't like."

"But this will make you rich," said Mr. Slate.

Fred put his arm around Wilma and lifted Pebbles into the air. "I was always the richest man in the world. I just didn't know it. So, if it's okay with you, all I want is my old job back. And my old life."

"Oh—and vacation time for every quarry worker," Fred said, remembering his promises. He looked at Barney. "And finally . . . those little packets of ketchup for the lunch area."

"Done!" said Mr. Slate. And he shook Fred's hand.

"I'm proud of you," Wilma told Fred as everyone headed to the car.

"I'm proud of you too," Betty said to Barney.

"And I'm starving," said Fred. "What do you say we get some breakfast? Snake and eggs for everyone. My treat."

Then Fred turned to Barney. "Could you spot me a couple of bucks?" he whispered. "I'm a little short."

Barney smiled. He had his old job back. His best friend was going to be working down at the quarry again. And best of all, Fred was asking him for a loan.

Everything was back to normal in Bedrock. The prehistoric town . . . in a prehistoric valley . . . by a prehistoric mountain . . . a long time ago in the prehistoric Stone Age.